The Sto

Hallsands

Chips Barber

OBELISK PUBLICATIONS

ALSO BY THE AUTHOR

The Story of Dawlish Warren
Around & About The Haldon Hills–Revisited • The Lost City of Exeter–Revisited
Diary of a Dartmoor Walker • Diary of a Devonshire Walker
The Great Little Dartmoor Book • The Great Little Exeter Book
The Great Little Plymouth Book • The Great Little Chagford Book
Dark and Dastardly Dartmoor • Weird and Wonderful Dartmoor
Ghastly and Ghostly Devon • The Ghosts of Exeter • Haunted Pubs in Devon
Ten Family Walks on Dartmoor • Six Short Pub Walks on Dartmoor
Ten Family Bike Rides in Devon
Railways On and Around Dartmoor • Devon's Railways of Yesteryear
Beautiful Exeter • Colourful Dartmoor • The South Hams in Colour
Topsham in Colour • Sidmouth in Colour • Dawlish and Dawlish Warren in Colour
Place-Names in Devon • An A to Z of Devon Dialect
Newton Ferrers and Noss Mayo
Down the Dart – Boat Trip from Totnes to Dartmouth
From the Dart to the Start • Dartmouth and Kingswear
Dartmouth of Yesteryear • Burgh Island and Bigbury Bay of Yesteryear
Around & About Burgh Island and Bigbury Bay
Around & About Hope Cove and Thurlestone
Walk the South Devon Coast–Dawlish Warren to Dartmouth
Walk the South Hams Coast–Dartmouth to Salcombe
Walk the South Hams Coast–Salcombe to Plymouth
Along The Avon

OTHER BOOKS ABOUT THIS AREA

Beesands and Hallsands of Yesteryear, *Cyril Courtney*
Beesands and Torcross of Yesteryear, *Cyril Courtney*
Walks in the South Hams, *Brian Carter*
Villages of the South Hams, *John Legge*
Churches of the South Hams, Parts I and II, *Walter Jacobson*

*We have over 200 Devon-based titles. For a list of current books please send SAE to
2 Church Hill, Pinhoe, Exeter, EX4 9ER. Tel: (01392) 468556.*

Acknowledgements
Thanks to Fred Lynn, Jill Norman and Cyril Courtney for their help and advice.

*First published in 2001, reprinted in 2002 and 2004 by
Obelisk Publications, 2 Church Hill, Pinhoe, Exeter, Devon
Designed and Typeset by Sally Barber
Printed in Great Britain by
Avocet Press, Cullompton, Devon*

The Story of Hallsands

Though England contains many odd nooks and corners, possibly none surpass the little village of Hallsands, the chief peculiarity of which is that it does not seem to possess a square foot of soil in the whole place. The visitor may look north and south along the curving lines of Start Bay and see plenty of green fields. Closer home, almost overhead, uprise the cliffs, which form the background of the village, breaking off into gentler slopes. But down in the village itself there is nothing but gravel and rock. The peculiarity of Hallsands is that it lies upon bare gravel, more or less compact, or else upon platforms of bare rock, just where the mile of steeply sloping grass which sweeps round from the Start gives place to a line of cliffs gradually increasing in height from 50 feet to the south of the village to 120 feet at the back of it, falling again further

northwards. The back of the village, consequently, consists of a natural wall rising to its greatest height about the centre of the village itself, and gradually falling off to right and left, whilst above this natural wall its rapid incline of grassy glacis leads the eye up to a very near horizon, having an average height of about 300 feet, and forming the backbone of the Start peninsula. The village of Hallsands itself looks as if it properly belonged to the sea, and had only been borrowed from it for a time. The whole of the platform on which the village stands is only from 30 to 40 feet wide, with a single row of cottages just under the cliffs, and a narrow road along which a van can pass until about the middle of the village, where it abruptly ends in the gravel.

Hallsands faces due east, and as it stands within a few yards of the sea, it is very exposed, and receives a fierce beating of sea and spray in a strong easterly gale. Up to within a few years ago the inhabitants held their own against the sea, by a long stretch of pebble beach that had formed in front of the village.

So wrote James Fairweather of Salcombe about a century ago in his guide to the neighbourhood.

Many others have been drawn, and felt moved, to write of this amazing place. This is a further account which differs, I hope, from some of the others by drawing largely upon the writings of those who witnessed the story of this storm-battered fishing village as it unfolded. Such contemporary accounts bring the 'tragedy' of Hallsands to life. These are the experiences of real

people who lived in an almost unreal situation. The shingle beach was their natural protection from the powerful wind-driven waves that came from the great open expanse of sea to the east. With this natural barrier intact the village was relatively safe; without it...

This book tells, largely by first-hand accounts, the unique story of how, through human folly, the waterside settlement of Hallsands was destroyed, the humble homes of the fishing community succumbing to the not-so-tender mercies of a sometimes cruel sea. It provided their livelihoods but given a mighty help by the hand of Man, one in particular, it also proved to be their doom.

What sort of place was Hallsands in its Victorian heyday? It was out on a geographical limb, the parish church of Stokenham a stiff walk or ride away over the hills. A jaunt into the nearest market town of Kingsbridge was not undertaken lightly. Comings and goings were most easily effected by sea-travel. The round trip, about 30 miles, to Dartmouth was an easier journey by water than it was over land. It still is!

Hallsands, with a population of about 150, was a small fishing village and as such was a close-knit community. The 1878 directory for Devon lists Philip Prettejohn as being the proprietor of the 'Hallsands Inn' and James Mingo as the baker. The latter was also listed, in 1897, as shopkeeper and owner of private apartments. The doors of the homes were rarely locked; everyone knew everyone else. There were certain long-established families and surnames almost peculiar to the district. This is the story of the Prettejohns, Mingos, Trouts, Lynns, Crockers, Steeres, Stones, Logans and Pateys as much as the story of the ill-fated village. These families lived what we would now regard as simple lives on the narrow, rocky ledge. Above them, atop the dark-coloured cliffs, there were terraces where allotments yielded vegetables and fruit. In some ways theirs was a 'Good Life'-styled existence but as the nineteenth century drew to a close a dark cloud appeared on the horizon.

An agreement was made on 10 November 1896 between the Board of Trade and Sir John Jackson. It gave the latter the licence to dredge and carry away sand, gravel, shingle and other material from the bed of the sea at Start Bay and opposite Hallsands and Beesands, within an area delineated on a plan attached to the licence. One of the terms stated that if the Board of Trade thought damage was occurring to the foreshore, the licence could be cancelled.

The exact wording of the indenture dated 10 December 1896, between the 'Queen's Most Excellent Majesty' of the first part, John Francis Fortescue Homer, a Commissioner of Woods, of the second part, and Sir John Jackson of the third part, authorised the latter to 'dig, dredge and carry away sand and shingle within, under, or upon the foreshore of the sea between high- and low-water marks at and opposite Hallsands and Beeson Sands'.

The following April saw the commencement of the dredging operation. Initially a bucket-ladder dredger was used. This was soon replaced by two suction-pump dredges.

From that moment on there was uproar; immense concern was shown by those who witnessed the scale of the operation. The local MP was quickly contacted. Mr Francis Bingham Mildmay asked a question in the House of Commons on the behalf of the locals.

Consequently the Board of Trade sent their representative, Captain Vereker, down to inspect the situation. He held an inquiry at Hallsands' coastguard station. The fishermen's representative was Mr Edward Windeatt of Totnes. He conjectured that if the shingle was removed, it would cause the bringing down of the houses at Hallsands. He put forward the argument that when the wind blew from the south-east, the wash on Hallsands beach would drag the beach material down into the void created by the dredging. He was right.

However, Sir John's representative argued that sand would fill the gap and thus the beach would be safe. *He* was wrong!

One fisherman wisely observed, 'What Sir John Jackson takes down to Devonport can never come back again.'

Given the evidence presented, the Board of Trade told Mr Mildmay that they would not withdraw the licence. This decision was ultimately to decide the fate of the village. But at least the point had been brought home to Sir John Jackson. In August 1897, through the intervention of Mr Windeatt, an agreement was achieved which saw that the fishermen of Hallsands were compensated to the tune of £125 per year for the interference of their fishing. Beesands received £48 on the same basis.

In real terms this compensation package worked out at £4 per year, per head, at Hallsands and £1.50 at Beesands. To show good faith, Sir John added Christmas gratuities of £20 to sweeten the situation.

And so the relentless dredging continued, hundreds of thousands of tons being sucked, scraped, gathered and removed to feed the insatiable needs of the concrete-making machinery used in the development of Keyham's dockyard at Devonport.

A HOPPER BEING FILLED WITH SHINGLE FROM THE BEACH.

The bulk of the dredging took place to the north of Hallsands, from a point just below the Bible Christian Chapel and towards Tinsey Head, about two-thirds of a mile away. The technique of removal was as follows. Sand, which was in abundance below the low-water mark, was not wanted. Therefore the suction dredgers, with a draught of four feet forward, eight feet aft, waited offshore as the tide began to flow in. The working period, as they followed the tide, lasted until it turned again. In that period they systematically assaulted the shoreline, moving the material into hopper barges. In a productive session two could be filled, but on most occasions just one – holding 1,100 tons – was loaded. The dredging went on, the removal of material cutting inside the original high-water mark of the beach.

Early in 1901, the sea-walls at the southern end of the village were undermined. Sir John funded the new concrete footings. The beach had dropped an alarming seven feet since the dredging operation had commenced. As predicted years earlier, the village's natural protection was fast disappearing into the sea.

The damage was all too apparent. Mr Mildmay, a most conscientious Member of Parliament, once again voiced his concerns. In September 1901 the Board of Trade, who had dismissed the earlier objections, sent their inspector, Captain Frederick, to re-examine the situation. To his credit he acknowledged the damage which had been done. The erosion of the beach was evident from Torcross all the way to Hareston Rock, to the south of the village. This was denudation on a major scale. So much for 'Nature' replacing the missing material. The Board of Trade duly restricted the area covered by the original licence. In January 1902 the licence was terminated, but the gesture was too late to spare Hallsands.

About 650,000 tons of material had been removed. One can imagine the mood of the fishermen when Sir John Jackson faced them at Torcross on 22 January 1902. He offered them a small amount of compensation. By an overwhelming majority they rejected his derisory offer. It is likely that they all knew, or at least suspected, what fate would befall Hallsands in the following few years. The winter of 1901–02 passed by without any major incidents. The following winter, however, was a different proposition.

This appeared in the press on 2 February 1903:

A close inspection of the little fishing village of Hallsands, situate between Torcross and Start Point Lighthouse, reveals the terrible havoc which has been caused by the recent heavy storms, and the imminent danger, should it be visited with another easterly gale, of the whole of the thirty houses of which it is composed, with their 150 inhabitants, of whom 36 are fishermen, owning 16 boats. Situated as it is on a narrow ledge or platform, on the side of a cliff about 150 feet high, and exposed to the full force of an angry sea, without the natural protection which was formerly afforded by the shingle beach, the position of the place is certainly so grave as to warrant some prompt steps being taken to avert what might be a serious disaster.

A representative of the *Western Morning News* visited the village yesterday, and had pointed out to him the effects of the late gale. The greatest damage has been caused at the further end towards Start Point. There stands in isolated ruin what up to a few days since was a fairly substantial four-roomed cottage, occupied by Miss Ann Trout. The whole of one side the house is gone. The sea, dashing up, undermined the walls and washed away the foundations, and then the end fell in, consisting of the larger portions of the upstairs and downstairs rooms, leaving the rafters and interior exposed. Quite one third of the house has disappeared. Fortunately the occupier was enabled to remove her furniture before the destruction was accomplished, and she has gone to live with her niece in another part of the village. The pathway which led to the cottage has also been washed clean away. Damage has likewise been caused to the cottage close by, occupied by William Trout, fisherman, in front of which the whole of the quay wall has been washed out for the second time within six weeks. The only protection afforded at the spot at present is a quantity of planks and furze. The next house, occupied by John Gillard, a farm labourer, formerly a fisherman, has also suffered. Owing to its being undermined by the action of the sea, he had to remove his furniture to another cottage, with his wife and two children. He had a very unpleasant experience, for the next morning, owing still to the inroads of the sea, he had again to move to another house. In front of the adjoining house there is a great crack in what is called the quay wall, which has sunk some six feet. The houses standing just behind are fairly safe whilst the wall remains standing, but in its weakened and shattered condition is not likely to be of long duration. Some 12 or 14 feet of the slipway, used by the fishermen for the last 23 years for hauling their boats up and down, has been washed away. Mr George Trout and his son, Harold, were on Sunday morning employed for an hour and a half up to their waists in water trying to keep the stones in the wall in position as they were being washed out by the sea; but for these timely exertions the probability is that the wall would have collapsed.

A portion of the front premises of the London Inn – the only public house in the village – has likewise been so undermined by the sea that the usual means of access to the front door has been cut off, and customers have to go through the cellar into the interior. The little conservatory put up last summer only stands by being shored up with planks from underneath. The landlord, who has only been in occupation of the house a couple of months, is Mr Lobb, a naval pensioner, formerly of Saltash. Where the quay wall has been more seriously undermined the fishermen have done their best to keep it intact by placing stones under the foundations, but this would be of very little service in the event of another big inroads of the sea...

The London Inn was built on a site which had been occupied since 1784. The earliest houses or homes in the village had taken advantage of some short spurs of rock to give them a firm foundation but there were also properties built half on the shingle. These were the first to go.

When the beach was intact, fishing boats could be kept on the beach all year round, but at the prospect of the severest storms they had to be removed to a safer haven. The slipway was an important feature.

Although the days got warmer and brighter, the winter of discontent continued. This appeared in the local press on 3 March 1903:

Our representative again visited Hallsands yesterday, and found that the havoc wrought by the gale is terrible. At the extreme west of the village a cottage was on Sunday morning so weakened by having its foundation sucked from under it that part of it has been completely swept away by the sea, and the other part remains standing on the very edge of the platform ready to wholly fall away the next time the tide comes in. One end of the village is completely isolated owing to the destruction of the road, and it is only possible to establish communication as the tide recedes far enough to walk to and fro on the sand below. Surveying the cottages from the sand gives one the impression that the whole place is crumbling and sinking down, and so fragile does it appear that one wonders why the place is not evacuated. The village has been showing signs of weakening for some time, but it was not until last Friday morning that any serious visible damage occurred. Most of the villagers had been up all night, fearing that with the heavy sea some part might be swept away. Unfortunately their fears proved only too well grounded. George Stone, a fisherman, was looking round the quays – as the space in front of the houses are called – for possible damage, with a lantern, and stepped onto the quay in front of the little Inn, when the surface gave away with him and he fell into a large hole, and but for his being a very powerful man must have been taken off shore by the out-rush of the water. The place had become undermined during the night. After this no one cared to explore very much until daylight came. The effect was then only too apparent. Practically all the masonry in the retaining walls had had the foundations washed away, and the whole foreshore of the village was in a state of collapse, all undermined.

Hansford Worth was called in, on 13 March 1903, to inspect and advise on the condition of Hallsands. Educated at Plymouth High School, he had many strings to his bow: in later life his book *Worth's Dartmoor* was described as 'a kingpin of Dartmoor literature, a classic'; he was a founder member of the Marine Biological Association of the United Kingdom, Member of the Newcomen Society and Fellow of the Geological Society of London. He was held in the highest esteem. He was also sympathetic to the plight of the villagers and from that time on acted as honorary engineering adviser to the fishermen. He calculated that the beach level had dropped by a frightening 11 feet over the entire area in front of Hallsands. He advocated that immediate measures should be taken to protect the village. He noted the various efforts of the locals to 'stem the tide' and the minor efforts afforded by Sir John Jackson to arrest the situation. He also spelt out most clearly that the worst was to come. In a bid to check the problems, the construction of a new sea-wall was commenced in July 1903 but in the immediate months following there was further destruction. On 24 August a south-east wind whipped up a frenzied sea which broke over the old sea-wall at the south end of the village.

Even worse was to follow in late September, traditionally one of the more benign months of the year. This is how the press covered the events of the previous day on the 21st of that month:

Hallsands is little known to the ordinary tourist. Truth to tell, its two lines of cottages, separated by a narrow and not very well made thoroughfare, offer no inducement to *paterfamilias* in search of a holiday resort for his wife and children. Besides, it is at least eight miles from the nearest railway station. To the robust individual, one who desires to study character as exemplified by honest, straightforward, God-fearing fishermen, then Hallsands is to be commended.

The small cluster of houses, numbering about thirty, built principally upon rocks beneath a towering cliff, presents a highly picturesque appearance. It is, in fact, a typical Devonshire fishing village, the houses being owned chiefly by the fishermen themselves. The foreshore belongs to the Government, and herein lies the terrible misfortune which overhangs the little community. When the Keyham Extension Works were commenced, many thousands of tons of gravel and shingles were required, and Hallsands was one of the places selected from which these materials were to be obtained. It must be confessed that no one foresaw – least of all the villagers – that the work of the dredger was likely to result in the destruction of private property. Indeed, so far from this being the case, the fishermen gladly accepted Sir John Jackson's award of £120 per annum during the three years the shingles were being removed, given not as the price of the materials, the ownership of which is invested in the Crown, but as compensation for the loss of fishing. Sir John also paid without demur claims for the loss of crab-pots, and when it was discovered that the huge excavations on the beach, representing the removal of between a half and three quarters of a million tons of shingles and sands, affected what is locally known as the quay, he had concrete fixed at the base of the wall.

Unfortunately, many months elapsed before it was found that serious mischief had been created. Houses commenced to crack, and the beach subsided to an alarming extent. It is estimated that the beach is now twenty feet lower than it was before dredging operations commenced. Houses formerly entered from the beach are now approached by steps, and the gravel bank upon which the fishermen used to pull up their boats in fairly rough weather, is now no more. As long ago as 1897, the Kingsbridge Rural District Council issued a notice warning the public that the road leading from the highland into the village was damaged and undermined by the action of the sea, and dangerous for all vehicular traffic, and it is therefore a little surprising that this beach should have been selected as the spot where to make gigantic excavations. What is still more incomprehensible is that, knowing the injurious effect which the removal of the sand bank has had upon private property, the authorities should still permit the wholesale carting away of the material. Yesterday afternoon men were observed loading a wagon, drawn by three horses, with shingles.

It was on New Year's-day, 1902, that the fishermen aroused themselves to take energetic action. They amalgamated with the men of Beesands, a village near by, also affected by the Government's action, and declared that they would not permit the dredger being used. The threat had the desired effect, and the dredger was seen no more on that part of the coast. The worst fears of the fishermen were realised in the spring of this year. A gale wrecked a cottage at the western end of the village, and to-day there is not a vestige of it to be seen. One half of the hamlet was completely cut off from the other portion at full tide, and communication was only restored when the tide receded. A substantial part of London Inn, the only licensed house in the community, had to be shored up with timber, and a little further on a cottage, built between two rocks, was so much damaged as to become uninhabitable. The miseries of the fishermen were voiced in Parliament by Mr Mildmay, member for the division, and as a result of his intervention a grant of £1000 was made by the Government to build a sea wall. The work has now been in operation some months, but the sum voted is totally inadequate for the needs of the place. So far only a wall of one hundred and fifty feet in length has been erected, under the superintendence of Mr Worth, engineer, of George-street, Plymouth, and there is fear that the work will come to a premature end through insufficient funds. This would be, indeed, a calamity. All the villagers are united in the belief that it was the new wall which saved the western end of the village in the great gale of Sunday night. The wall is built of concrete, having a width of seven feet at the foundation and two feet at the top, while its height ranges from twenty one feet to twenty four feet.

The past bitter experiences of the fishermen prepared them for something unusual on Sunday. On Saturday the tide was exceptionally high, and some resolved to wait up all night and keep watch. Nothing beyond the moaning of the wind, the roaring of the seas, and the beating of small stones upon the window panes disturbed the tranquillity of the night. At five o'clock on Sunday morning, however, there commenced the first equinoctial gale of the season, accompanied by a growing spring tide. It brought the sea far beyond its usual mark, sending spray into the narrow thoroughfare. The wind increased during the day, making an exceedingly heavy surf roll. Heavy breakers rolled continuously between 8 a.m. and 7.30 p.m., and cleared away the foundations of that portion of the London Inn which suffered so severely in the spring, causing it to collapse with startling rapidity. This section of the building comprised a cellar, kitchen, bedroom and loft, used as a store for fishermen.

The story of the catastrophe is, perhaps, best told in the words of Mr Lobb, the unfortunate landlord of the London Inn. He said: "When the greenhouse collapsed, two coastguardmen and two fishermen came to assist me to remove the things in the bedroom. While we were in the room the roof came down upon us, and we all had a narrow escape. Then the gable gave way, tearing away the stove and nearly blinding us with dust. It was with the greatest difficulty that we grasped things to prevent us from falling into the surf. My wife also had a very narrow escape. We had arranged to have tea, as usual, in the kitchen. Mrs Lobb was sitting down when the wall gave way, but not in her customary place, otherwise she would certainly have fallen and perished in the surf. We hurriedly removed all articles of furniture, and had just got out the last, when the whole pile went like a pack of cards. The noise and the dust was bewildering, the latter enveloping the assistants and myself. I heard the bystanders shout 'What has become of the men?'

"I should like especially to speak of the services of Mr Bidgwood, the foreman of the sea wall works. If it had not been for him and the work for which he has charge, the calamity would have been far greater. Entire communication with the other end of the village must have been cut off. Mr Bidgwood worked throughout Sunday morning with his men and a number of volunteers. He got some timber, faggots, and heavy stones, and placed them in such a position as to prevent loose stones running out to sea. I regret to say, however, that upwards of £10 worth of timber was lost, and that Mr Bidgwood himself completely spoilt the clothes he was wearing.

"Everything went before the tide as easily as a shuttlecock. I should have said that a temporary bridge erected for the convenience of customers early in the day gave way. We secured that in the surf, and fastened it up with strong ropes. On the gale increasing in violence it again gave way, and this time it went out to sea. Even the stove, which I regarded as the best thing in the house, was destroyed. I had a dozen or so empty cider casks in the cellars, but these were removed to a place of safety. The windows were protected by boards."

THE QUAY WALL AS IT WAS.

At the rear of the public house, separated only by a few feet of ground, is a cottage occupied by Mrs Stone. The building is not an old one – it was built for Mr Stone's mother when she became married – but, nevertheless, great fears were entertained for its safety. There was no rest in the household either on Saturday or Sunday night. Shingles beat upon all the windows facing the sea, and the situation became so alarming on Sunday night that everything was packed ready for instant flight. "Two heavy seas," said Mrs Stone, "would have levelled the place."

The cottage damaged so seriously last spring is now a total wreck. It looks curious, sandwiched between houses occupied but with windows barricaded to prevent them being broken by heavy seas. There is a strong feeling in Hallsands that the sea wall should be extended along those parts now exposed to the full force of an easterly or south-easterly gale. At least a dozen cottages are in imminent danger of being washed away in the first heavy storm, and something should be done quickly if they are to be saved.

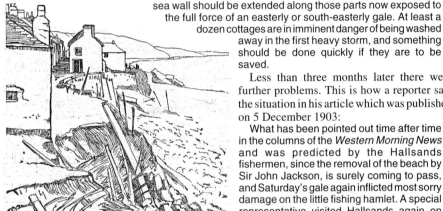

THE QUAY WALL AS IT IS.

Less than three months later there were further problems. This is how a reporter saw the situation in his article which was published on 5 December 1903:

What has been pointed out time after time in the columns of the *Western Morning News* and was predicted by the Hallsands fishermen, since the removal of the beach by Sir John Jackson, is surely coming to pass, and Saturday's gale again inflicted most sorry damage on the little fishing hamlet. A special representative visited Hallsands again on Monday afternoon, and, although it was perfectly apparent that the village had had a terrific battering, the fisherman were anxious to give their experiences of Saturday last.

The damage up to Saturday last had been mostly confined to the west side and middle of the village, but now two cottages, at almost the extreme and east end (immediately below the road which enters the village) have been practically demolished, and a third one adjoining is in immediate danger; all access is cut off from it, and it is isolated; whilst the earth and gravel have been sucked out almost up to its walls. All these cottages were some considerable distance back from the beach itself; they were built on one of the quays typical to the place, the quay being kept in position by a most solid and substantial wall. The wall was about 3 foot thick at the bottom end and up to about halfway was of concrete, the upper half of it was constructed of ordinary masonry, and it narrowed at the top to the thickness of about 18 inches, its length along the foreshore was about 70 ft, and was constructed principally by the villagers some years ago. The whole of this quay and wall has entirely disappeared, taking with it a large wooden boat slip, some outhouses, and the stable in which the Kingsbridge carrier, Harriet Stone, keeps her pony. Harriet Stone's house is the one completely isolated, all the furniture is removed, and she is finding other quarters in the village.

The two other houses adjoining which have had such a battering were occupied by William Logan, his wife, and seven children; and Robert Logan (father), his wife, and a grown-up son. The late domiciles of the Logans present a most desolate appearance. The front walls are entirely gone, leaving the whole of the interior visible; the roof has partially collapsed, and the ground floor overhangs the chasm in front, held together by the joists. All the furniture has luckily been saved, although some, on which apparently most value was set, has been badly smashed up. Strangely enough, the back of Robert Logan's house is still considered habitable, and this family are still occupying the kitchen and one bedroom, although, as has been pointed out, the front walls of the place are entirely gone. The Logans' houses are owned by Mr Bucknill, of Kellaton. The fisherman are most disconsolate and distracted over their ill-luck, and complain bitterly of the law which, they say, has permitted one man to come and deprive them of their natural breakwater and render so many homeless and dejected. William Logan has found accommodation for the time with his fishing partner, Lynn; Lynn's house is very small, and it can be imagined to what extent it is overcrowded.

The Logans gave the following account of Saturday's disaster: "it had been blowing hard from the SE all day, and in the afternoon the seas came tumbling in, shaking everything all to pieces. We became greatly alarmed, and happily took the precaution to remove our furniture in anticipation of what would happen. Harriet Stone was at Kingsbridge, and we telegraphed to her asking her to return at once. She came during the afternoon in time, with help, to get all our goods out. Instead of abating, as we hoped it would, the gale increased, and we soon saw that our cottages would come down. Huge waves rolled in from the Channel, bringing with them large stones which acted like battering rams to our quay wall. It withstood it for several hours, but about midnight it gave way, and in about half an hour the quay and all that stood on it was sucked away like feathers, and the front of our houses fell out. We at this time had no place to go, and we made the reading-room our headquarters, in which there was a nice fire burning."

While giving this account Logan was engaged in carrying from the beach up to a store the last of his property remaining to be salved. It consisted of a cradle and two children's chairs, and added not a little to the general scene of disaster and misery. During Saturday night, from 12 to three especially, the village itself seemed part of the sea. Most of the windows were shuttered, and in cases where this precaution was not taken the glass has been cracked and smashed up by the gravel thrown up by the waves.

At the London Inn all ways of communication have been cut off, and the corner of the house is standing on a piece of rock, from which all the masonry, which formed a kind of facing and supported a road, has been washed. The wall erected in front of the chasm caused by a preceding gale, and about which there is now so much quibbling as to payment, has stood the gale and looks uninjured, although the chasm at the back of it was full of water for several hours, and it was at the time getting a fearful battering from outside. The water inside the wall has had the effect of narrowing the road still more, and it had now diminished to about five feet six inches, and it is certain that unless this chasm is filled up before another gale comes, the road will entirely disappear, and the row of cottages immediately at the back be in imminent danger. An expert with our representative had no hesitation in stating that unless the filling was put at the back off the wall, he should not like to answer for it, if a similar battering to which it had been subjected occurred again.

As for showing the fury of the sea on Saturday, a fisherman pointed out several blocks of concrete taken from the old quays – each weighing some tons, and left lying on the beach – which had been shifted several yards. He also mentioned that had the gale taken place on a spring tide instead of a low neap, the devastation must have been much more severe.

It is stated that the beach is now lower than ever, and it is accounted for by the fact that the pits caused by the dredging are now filling up, and that the whole is sinking to a much lower level than it ever has been before. This it is asserted, is the case all along the bay. This is an additional hardship to the inhabitants as it is feared that when net fishing is again tried it will be found impossible, owing to rocks which were formerly buried in gravel now projecting through the bottom, in which the gear will hang and tear. The villagers say they have known worse gales before the removal of the shingle, when no damage was done, and if it sinks much lower they express the fear that some day they will be washed out like rats from a hole.

This was a tough winter and the weather was to continue to prove unkind to the villagers of Hallsands. Every time they thought there was some respite, the conditions contrived to remind them of the precarious position in which they found themselves. January 1904 passed by peacefully but February saw a return of the troubles. This was reported on 19 February:

On Tuesday night and Wednesday morning the south-east wind blowing, with the high spring tides, wrought considerable damage at Hallsands, causing great hardship, misery, and fear amongst the inhabitants. The huge waves sent sea and spray over the tops of almost all the houses and cottages, large volumes of water descending through the chimneys, while shingle and sand battered against the windows with great force. The new sea-wall was almost useless, the waves rushing in with such force that the whole pressure went scores of feet over it and dashed against the buildings. A parish road at the north entrance to the village was completely washed away, thus cutting off all connection between one end and the other.

Through this huge waves curled round, and there is every probability of the well known pit recently filled in being sucked away. That would again endanger the main road outside the London Inn. It was stated freely in Dodbrooke Market on Wednesday that Torcross was threatened and should a south-easterly gale spring up disastrous will be the results all along the coast, including that village, as well as Beesands. Many at Hallsands were obliged to leave their dwellings and seek refuge elsewhere. It is considered that the continual dredging off the Skerries is, if anything, more disastrous than dredging Start Bay, as it is believed that if that had not been done the shingle and sand would have returned in course of time to the beach along the coast, and thus have formed the natural breakwater. Not within living memory has there been such a terrible visitation of the South Devon coast as was experienced on Friday and Saturday when a furious south-east gale raged for several hours, and, combined with an abnormally high tide which rose some four or five feet above the maximum, wrought serious havoc at Torcross, Hallsands and other places. Hallsands suffered the most severely as was only to be expected, as the little fishing village lies close to the sea shore and is entirely without protection. It fell an easy prey to the tremendous seas which rolled in and dashed against the homes of the fisher-folk. At one time there was a fine shingle beach here, which acted as a kind of barrier, but large quantities of the shingle was removed some years ago for constructing concrete blocks for Keyham extension works. A sea wall was afterwards erected, when it was seen that the village had been exposed to serious danger, and in fact, some of the houses were at one time wrecked by the encroaching sea. But the damage done then was small compared with the ruin occasioned on Saturday.

There were lighter moments in the face of adversity and also proof that every cloud, however dark and threatening, has a silver lining. At the height of this storm, when the waves were going over the top of his house, down the chimney and back out through the front door, a villager made the observation that at least he wouldn't be requiring the services of the chimney sweep!

March roared in like a lion. This report featured in the press during the first week of that bleak month for Hallsands:

The recent easterly winds prevailing in the Channel have brought Hallsands one step nearer final demolition, and it is difficult to imagine the abject misery which at present prevails amongst the inhabitants through no fault of their own. By the action of the sea the village is now divided into three parts, each completely isolated from the other. The main road at the extreme foot of the cliff leads into the centre portion, and if a journey is to be made to the eastern portion a 30-foot ladder has to be descended to the beach, ending in a walk along the foreshore. This means of communication is only available at low-water. The difficulty of the villagers of this part of the hamlet may be imagined when it is realised that all domestic necessaries have to be brought to the houses along the way described. Should the inhabitants of any cottage be caught in this portion when a gale is on, one shudders at the result. The only possible escape would be a rope let down from the top of the cliffs immediately to the rear. Communication from the central portion to the westward end of the village is by a wooden bridge, recently erected over the chasm caused by the collapse of the parish wall. This western end, as the effect of Saturday's battering, is almost again subdivided, a few yards of soil at present being all that is left of the road.

Our correspondent visited Hallsands yesterday to see the effect of an easterly breeze at high water, and, although the fishermen said there was no sea on, and it was nothing, huge waves broke against the walls and torrents of water shot up against the houses and into the village street, carrying with it shingle and stones. There is scarcely a cottage which has not some damage to record, and as the result of Saturday and Sunday's gales it has been necessary to abandon five more. The most serious is the case of Mrs Logan, a widow lady over 70 years of age, who owned one of the nicest little abodes in the centre of the village with a neat garden in front. She shared its occupancy with her nephew and his wife. She tearfully stated how very hard it was, after a lifetime of thrift, to have her abode washed down, and she, but for the hospitality of her neighbours, to be homeless. The cottage is a complete wreck. The garden wall is down, the garden is a chasm, and the front of the house has entirely disappeared, leaving the whole of the interior exposed. The piece of wall that faced all this was on the seaward side of the road, and known as the parish wall, over which the Kingsbridge Rural Council have been debating for some time. Had that wall been promptly rebuilt the cottage at the back of it would have been saved. The next worst is three cottages further to the westward and directly opposite the village shop. These cottages are partly on rock and partly on soil. Where there is no rock the road has been defended by another wall, also owned by

the parish. On Saturday morning this wall began to give way at the bottom, and there was soon a big hole through which the road began to disappear, and there is now a chasm which extends a considerable distance across to the opposite house – the shop already mentioned. Until this last gale, all the cottages involved have been directly in front of the shore: but Mrs Logan's abode was situated on the opposite side of the street, and unless these two parish walls were rebuilt before the next breeze, some eight or 10 more cottages will collapse. Of the three cottages now rendered untenable, one is inhabited by Emma Sture (widow), her daughter, and son; the second by George Stone and his wife; and the third by Robert Steere, his wife, child, and an old lady, Anne Trout, in her 76th year. Anne Trout's cottage was the first cottage in the village to be washed away, and she has since been living with the Steeres.

Interviewed, Robert Steere said: "About 4.30 on Saturday morning we were awakened by the roaring of the sea and the waves leaping up to our windows. We became alarmed and were on the alert for the worst. Unfortunately our fears were well grounded, for soon the quay wall commenced to give way, followed by a part of the road. We barricaded our windows with boards, but the sea came up and tore it away in no time. Then in came the glass. We thought that would happen, and had pulled our bed and bedding as far as possible away from the window. It was no good, however. The sea came right into the bedroom windows, saturated our bedding and most of our furniture. We lost no time in clearing all this out; but our principal difficulty was with Anne Trout. We let her stay in the house until the last, feeble as she was, she had to go. The sea now commenced to rip the thatch off the roof, and the water poured down in torrents. From there and through the windows the water got so great we had to bore holes in the bedroom floor to let it down into the kitchen, and in the kitchen we made another hole in the side of the wall, for the water to escape again into the sea."

The Steeres' cottage presented a most dreary aspect. The shutters had again been nailed up. All the furniture was out of the house except a stool, on which Steere, his wife, and child were sitting in front of a fire just lit in the stove. The experience of Emma Steere and George Stone, who live in this same block, were very similar to those already given. Emma Steere's front door faces seaward, and that was barricaded from the inside, and boards nailed across the durns on the outside. It was of no avail. The whole lot was demolished and the house flooded in no time. All the furniture was saved, as finally the occupants made their exit by a bedroom window and a ladder at the back. George Stone's front door was also smashed in, but he had another entrance at the back, and that was found convenient in moving the furniture and fighting the waves in the way by keeping up the barricades when the tide was at its height. These three cottages were purchased by their present occupiers almost two years ago at an average cost of £115 each.

It is asserted that on Saturday the village was practically invisible through the sea and spray running over the houses. There is scarcely a sound roof in the whole place, the water having torn adrift the thatch and smashed the slates, pouring down through on to all the belongings. Even the plaster had been battered off the walls of most of the cottages, leaving the bare stone in sight. The water rushed in with such force that in some cases the durns of the doors were torn out. There is very little sound glass left in the place.

The new sea wall shows signs of the battering. In one place the foundation has started, and it is now possible to look underneath. In another place, such has been the action of the shingle on it, there is a hollow about eight inches deep.

What can be done? Even if a new sea wall stands, the houses, if they do not collapse, can be scarcely considered habitable, when with every little breeze water pours down the chimney, roofs are torn off, and the interiors inundated. It is marvellous how the villagers still hang on. But where can they go? If the fishermen go inland they must give up their occupations as fishermen. Mr Widger, of Beeson Farm, on Saturday sent a wagon to the village and offered any of the inhabitants who had been distressed, both lodging and storage for their furniture. Several availed themselves of his kindness. Overcrowding at Hallsands must soon become very serious, and unless another village is speedily built, it is difficult to know where accommodation will be found.

The houses lately vacated by Robert Logan and his son William at the extreme east end of the village, and damaged in a former gale, completely disappeared on Saturday. The matter is all the harder for the fishermen as their misfortunes are entirely the result of the dredging. They complain most bitterly that they should have to undergo such hardships and losses at the hands of those who were responsible for this, and assert that they should be compensated, if only to the extent of a decent habitation in which to reside. Considering the recent grants, however, it is difficult to see where the compensation is to come from, as the Board of Trade and Sir John Jackson (Limited) appear to have done all they intend to. The only possible aid seems to be by public subscription.

No doubt many of the villagers felt the worst of the weather was over as the winter mellowed into spring. Alas, in early May there was another terrible and terrifying storm. This is how it was reported on 7 May 1904:

As the result of the south-easterly gale on Saturday and yesterday what remained of the village of Hallsands has been almost swept away. Should there be a recurrence of the storm little will be left. The main quay, known as Mingle's, has been quite demolished, leaving no connection at the opposite end, which can only be approached by means of a narrow plank. The waves swept over the whole place and reached far above the main street of the village. Families residing in the few remaining dwellings have had their goods packed for some weeks in readiness to leave at any moment. Most of these have left their homesteads to the mercy of the waves, which have destroyed many of them. The London Inn – hitherto withstanding the force of the sea through being built upon a rock – has now collapsed, and little remains of the ancient hostelry of the place. It has been gradually undermined by the force of the sea beating against and inside the house, huge boulders having been forced against it as well as shingle and sand. The new sea wall, although somewhat breaking the force of the waves, is considered practically useless to protect the village, volumes of water simply rearing several feet above it and flooding the whole area behind.

After the serious devastations of Saturday nothing remains but to let the whole place go and rebuild the village higher up. To attempt anything else would be throwing money away. There is not a safe place in which to take shelter and any time the few remaining cottages may topple down. Large numbers visited that place yesterday. Many of the villagers are practically homeless. They cannot reside at any great distance away, as it is important they should be near their work.

A Hallsands visitor writing our Salcombe correspondent on Saturday says: "We had a fearful time here this morning up to 11 o'clock. So much sea on: a lot of damage done. Already, abreast of the shop part of the road is gone, and part of the old wall. The people are removing their furniture. Some are going to Beesands to sleep tonight. They are afraid to stop in their houses. For tonight I am offered a bed at Beesands, and shall accept if the sea does not go down. I do not care to risk it here I cleared out this morning and went to Beesands for a few hours. From the hill I saw the spray go 30 or 40 feet above the highest part of the village. It is heart-rending to see the poor women, and the men I think are quite unnerved." Instead of the wind abating on Saturday night it increased, with the result that a lot more damage was done.

Access to Hallsands is simply across a plank in front of the doorstep of Mr Robert Logan, whose house is so undermined as to make even that means unsafe. Mr Logan complains that he was wrongfully accused of refusing leave to Mr Lobb to take eight casks of ale across it to his place of business in the stable. He states he told Mr Lobb he could carry the casks across but was afraid the vibration of rolling them would seriously injure what was already in a very critical condition. The plank is the only means of getting to the village, and only of sufficient strength for a person to walk over.

To Kingsbridge Rural District Council on Saturday, Mr W. Beer, clerk, read a letter from the Board of Trade stating that for the past four months only two loads of sand had been taken from the Skerries, according to information from Sir John Jackson, and that no more would now be taken. – Mr J. Balkwill, surveyor, reported that the roads at Hallsands were extremely bad, and he hardly knew what to do, as the sea was washing right over Greenstraight. – Mr R. B. Prettejohn reported that the visit of the Committee appointed resulted in Mr Worth C.E., being asked to give an estimate of the cost of erecting a new concrete wall. They had a long meeting, and were at their wits' end really to know what was best to do. The decision arrived at was unanimous – the clerk said Mr Worth's estimates for a new parish wall was £100, the road being from 12 to 10 ft wide. – Mr Prettejohn: the wall would be built inside the line of the road. – Mr J. Balkwill looked upon it as virtually rebuilding a new quay for the people. Plans produced were closely scanned by the councillors. – the Chairman (Mr T. Adams) observed that for some time past they had been constantly told that Hallsands was doomed, and was bound to go altogether. If that were so, more money spent would be practically thrown away. He would do anything to help in the present condition of affairs, but should well consider the matter before spending £100. – Mr W. Worth did not see why they should spend the money if the council was not liable. Enough had already been thrown away. He moved that they do not entertain the recommendation. – Mr J. Cornish seconded. – Mr P. Cole (of Stokenham): something must be done. – Rev W. D. Bateman said the evidence adduced as to the durability or otherwise of the village had been of a very conflicting character. – Mr R. Rogers said although a deal of money had been spent, he believed if the proposed work were done it would save the village for many years. It would, however, have been best if the village had been rebuilt in the first place. That was not the work of the committee but of some other authority. – Mr Symons considered it imperative that something be done at once, and suggested sending the plan and estimate to the Board of Trade. – In reply to the question, the Surveyor said the council had already spent £50 on the place. That had nothing to do with the sea wall. – Mr Prettejohn: It will take a long time to get a reply from the Board of Trade. Why not write Sir John Jackson? – Mr Honeywill: The question is what is to be done in the meantime: – Mr Cole considered £50 would build the quay wall, and Mr Prettejohn suggested they invite tenders for the work. – The Surveyor said the road would be 10 feet wide into the village road of 8 feet. – For sending to the Board of Trade eight voted for, four against. – Mr P. Cole moved asking for tenders at once. – Mr Prettejohn seconded, observing that the villagers were in a most distressing state. Delay would make the position worse. – This was lost, and it was ultimately decided to send the plan and estimate to the Board of Trade, asking for immediate attention and a reply.

The *Western Morning News*, who had taken such a great interest in this long-drawn-out saga, realised that many villagers were still homeless. To solve the problem they established a public subscription, which realised £650, to be spent on properties 'well beyond the reach of the sea'.

The long-term safety of the waterfront village was a matter of great debate and the winning of compensation for the villagers was, as it always is, a long-drawn-out affair. Fortunately they had their champions, people with power and influence and, perhaps more importantly, the determination to fight their corner.

If you have made your own opinions based on the circumstances presented so far, then you will have probably reached the same conclusions as the majority of local folk. However, it suited Sir John Jackson to see it rather differently. The Board of Trade supported him. They wrote to the Kingsbridge Rural District Council stating that the conditions prevalent in the village were largely attributable to 'natural causes'. When Sir John Jackson spoke at Devonport he asserted a similar belief, but added that he presumed 'ninety-nine persons out of a hundred would find it difficult to believe.' Hansford Worth, a skilled and intuitive engineer, knew better. He cited several reasons why Sir John and the Board of Trade were wrong. Consequently, the sum of £1,000 was offered in April 1903, jointly by the Board of Trade and Sir John Jackson, as compensation to all those who had suffered damage from the drop in beach level at Hallsands.

On the 29th of that month the offer was accepted by the majority of those present at the meeting.

However the conditions which were attached to it – the recipients should give 'a full and final receipt in full and final settlement of all claims' – posed its inevitable problems to those wary of making such an irrevocable declaration.

Fortunately, before anything was signed there was a realisation that the amount on offer was completely inadequate. The offer was thus increased to £1,750, and in June 1904 to £3,250. Mr Mildmay, keen to see a settlement, generously added £250 to this figure. However, as the owner of the London Inn had instituted proceedings against Sir John Jackson Limited, the offer was reduced by £250 to cover any contingencies in this direction.

Immense damage had been done to Hallsands but there were no major incidents in the following years. The new sea-wall held firm, the wind behaved itself, and things began to improve. Life returned to some form of quiet normality for those who stayed. Thanks to the weather pattern, Hallsands was out of the news and glad to be so.

For more than a decade, the dreaded 'double-act' of a high spring tide driven on by a stiff easterly wind was noticeable by its welcomed absence. But those who understood patterns of weather, and who knew the whims of wind and tide, believed that sooner or later it would happen again. They also appreciated that without the all-important shingle ridge, Hansford Worth's sea-wall – however well built – would not save the village in a major storm.

All was well until late January 1917. Part of the philosophy of those who lived 'like limpets attached to the very rock' at Hallsands was that there would be 'time enough to leave when their houses left them!' This adage was about to be sorely examined. This report appeared on the 29th of that fateful month and told of the horrendous happenings of a few days earlier. The villagers' worst nightmare became stark reality:

Not within living memory has there been such a terrible visitation of the South Devon coast as was experienced on Friday and Saturday, when a furious south-east gale raged for several hours, and, combined with an abnormally high tide which rose some four or five feet above the maximum, wrought serious havoc at Torcross, Hallsands and other places. Hallsands suffered the most severely as was only to be expected, as the little fishing village lies close to the sea shore and is entirely without protection. It fell an easy prey to the tremendous seas which rolled in and dashed against the homes of the fisher folk. At one time there was a fine shingle beach here, which acted as a kind of barrier, but large quantities of the shingle was removed some years ago for constructing concrete blocks for Keyham Extension Works. A sea wall was afterwards erected, when it was seen that the village had been exposed to serious danger, and in fact, some of the houses were at one time wrecked by the encroaching sea. But the damage done then was small compared with the ruin occasioned on Saturday.

The storm burst on Friday evening and the people living on the seashore very soon saw that their houses were doomed. They speedily made their way to a place of safety at the top of the cliff, but one old lady who was an invalid, could not be removed until the following day. Such was the fury of the waves that the householders found it difficult to save much of their belongings, and some have lost the whole of their goods and chattels.

When morning broke a scene of desolation presented itself to the eye. The fishing boats had been tossed up clean into the meadows, wreckage was strewn about in all directions, and the village was practically wiped out. The seas swamped right over the houses, which seemed to crumple beneath their weight. Some of the people had a terrible experience. In one case there were nine people huddled together in a little house against which the waves were incessantly dashing, and they were expecting every moment that the walls which afforded them shelter would collapse, and that they would be washed away. They had to bore holes in the bedroom floor to let the water down into the kitchen. It was impossible to save anything in the place, or for them to make their escape until the tide went out. One of the fishermen, James Lynn, saw two huge waves crash against his house and knock most of the front of it clean in. The lamp was extinguished, and the people were in utter darkness, but they managed to make their escape by the back door. Another house nearby was levelled to the ground, and the roofs of others have been lifted off. Altogether 24 families have been rendered homeless. One old fisherman, sorrowfully viewing the wreckage on Saturday, said "This is the end of our village. We shall have to go elsewhere."

The twin village of Beesands, which lies in the direction of Torcross, has also little protection from the sea, and it suffered severely, although not to the same extent as Hallsands. The people, when they saw they were in for a rough time on Friday night, did their best to barricade their premises. Several houses were much damaged, however, and at one end of the hamlet the roadway has disappeared, and also part of a garden. The Mission Church, which was erected some years ago by Miss Theresa Jones, of Totnes, is uninjured.

Torcross also felt the full force of the gale. The place was inundated, and extensive damage has been done at The Lea. The magnificent sea drive, which runs for miles along the shore, has disappeared, and the Lake parallel to it has been converted into a large swamp. The

inhabitants, realising their peril, were able to make their escape inland.

It was a time for further recriminations. The story, so well-documented and publicised years earlier, had reached its inevitable conclusion. Hallsands, in terms of its rock-ledge properties, had been destroyed. It was now a case, once again, of how best to seek and acquire compensation. This again was no easy matter as the Board of Trade still maintained that 'natural causes' led to the village's destruction. It also reminded the villagers of their 1904 'in full and final settlement' agreement.

In the meanwhile, some moved away, others lived with friends or relatives, and the less fortunate had to 'rough it'. Five men spent several months sleeping in a loft over a coachhouse. Some folks were even reduced, on warmer nights, to sleeping in the ruins of their former homes.

The *Western Morning News*, which had covered the Hallsands story in close detail for 20 years, stepped in once more to fly the flag for the villagers' plight. By their full coverage and well-written editorials, they brought pressure to bear on the authorities. Even the hard-nosed Board of Trade conceded the request for an independent inquiry. Consequently the sum of £6,000 was eventually made available in May 1919, more than two years after the disaster. Of this £2,000 was allocated to paying for lost furniture, clothing and so on. The balance was not a sufficiently large sum to rebuild the village on its original site, so an inland spot was sought. Mr A. E. Spender, editor of the *Western Morning News*, generously donated £200 out of his own pocket towards the cost of the new homes.

In 1924, ten new houses, Fordworth Cottages, became home to those who had been displaced seven years earlier. The choice of name for this long line of homes, was an amalgam of two of the prime supporters for the village, Richard Hansford Worth and H. Ford, who was clerk to the Fisheries Committee. Another six houses were later added.

This was how the press covered the work in progress on 10 April 1923:

Considerable progress has been made in rebuilding the fishing village of Hallsands, near Plymouth, which was destroyed by a gale in 1917. An interesting little ceremony took place when Mr E. C. Perry (Chairman of the Devon Sea Fisheries Committee) laid a stone commemorating the rebuilding. Largely as a result of the efforts of the committee, sufficient funds have been raised to erect 10 cottages, four of which are well on the way to completion. The Board of Trade paid £6,000 in compensation (for removal of shingle for Keyham Dockyard extension), £2,000 of which was allocated to make good personal losses. A public utility society was formed, and a loan of £3,623 obtained from the Public Works Loan Board.

Mr Perry said two men stood out prominently in the matter – Mr R. Hansford Worth, who from the first had thrown himself into the cause of the fishermen with zeal and ability, and had done yeoman work, and Mr H. Ford, the clerk to the Sea Fisheries Committee. They greatly regretted that Lord Mildmay, through ill-health, was unable to be with them, but he (Mr Perry) had received a letter in which his Lordship wrote: "May all go well with Hallsands in future." Lady Mildmay had written "I am so delighted that the fruits of all your labours in connection with the scheme have resulted so successfully."

Thanks to Mr Perry were voiced by Mr G. Trout, a local fisherman, on behalf of the villagers, and endorsed by Mr W. J. Sanders, who said Hallsands had had the sympathy of all the surrounding country.

Mr Ford and Mr G. Windeatt, also spoke, Mr G. Windeatt expressing the hope that the fishermen would soon own their own cottages.

At the conclusion of the ceremony, a couple of fishermen appeared with a basket containing some huge crabs and a lobster, which they presented to the members of the committee as a token of appreciation for all that had been done.

Mr T. B. Prettejohn, a member of the committee, who was unable to be present, entertained the members to lunch at Torcross prior to the ceremony.

In 1964 these properties were modernised to make more comfortable homes, with indoor lavatories, bathrooms and hot-water systems introduced. This enhancement scheme cost £14,000.

The village was in the limelight again, for a completely different reason, in 1917:

A Devonshire Grace Darling was revealed as a result of questions put in the House of Commons. Ella Trout, aged 20, of Hallsands, with her cousin, aged 10, was fishing for mackerel off the Start on 8 September when the safety of the boat was endangered by an explosion. A steamer a mile distant was then seen to be on the point of going down. Fearless of the submarine, the girl lowered the sails, and rowed to the scene of the disaster. Wind and tide retarded her, so that the steamer had sank. Rowing through the wreckage, she came across only one of the crew – a man of colour. He was rescued, resuscitated, and handed over to a patrol boat.

This heroine of the South Hams is, with her sister, the main support of a widowed mother. Their cottage was one of those destroyed by the gale at the opening of the present year. The facts, as stated to the Board of Trade, certainly disclose a remarkable degree of courage, presence of mind, and promptness in action. Pulling an almost drowned man into the boat was in itself a task of enormous difficulty, yet this was accomplished by the girl herself whilst the boy tried to keep the boat steady. After this she had to row further out in search of a patrol boat. Fortunately eight of the crew were rescued by a Salcombe motorboat fishing in the vicinity.

Her effort was recognised by a local bard who penned these words in her honour, this being titled *A Ballad of Hallsands Bay.*

Calm is the sea and clear the air,
The dimpling wavelets landward stray,
A little boat that takes no share
In war's implacable array;
A child and maiden oar her crew,
Puts forth on such a peaceful day,
When Londoners express their view
There is no war down Devon way.

Athwart their course the waters bear
A wreck that staggered rent and grey,
With one yet clinging In despair,
Survivor of the treach-rous fray.
He gazed upon the open blue,
Tasted the bitter salted spray,
Nor any hope of succour knew –
There is no war down Devon way.

To snatch the victim from the snare
She plied her oar with even sway,
Unfaltering, although aware
Of grim occasion for dismay:
A lurking monster might pursue,
Speeding in search of further prey,
And all the sea with blood imbrue –
There is no war down Devon way.

Envoi

This verse is but a tribute due
To Ella Trout, of Hallsands Bay,
Since it is thanks to yours and you
There is no war down Devon way.

Ella Trout was undoubtedly a very brave lady. It has been widely reported that the parents of the young man she rescued gave her a sum of money as a thank-you gesture, with which she purchased a clifftop site, near to the road which led down to the old village of Hallsands. However, although she did indeed acquire the land, a member of her family assures me that this was not as a result of any monetary reward for her brave deed.

Ella and Patience, one of her three sisters, set to work to dig out the foundations for this large building which was initially called Prospect House. In addition to this they plumbed in the water supply and even made the concrete blocks from which the building was to be constructed. Their resolve was probably strengthened by the fact that they and their widowed mother, Eliza Ann, had been made homeless by the 1917 storm.

The new property was large enough for them to be able to offer letting rooms to guests. The Trouts made a success out of the venture and the small guest house was, in 1933, developed into the Prospect House Hotel, which could accommodate almost 70 guests when full. The success of the enterprise, as is usually the case, was achieved with repeat business – visitors coming back year after year. Needless to say, fish dishes were the speciality.

THIS FOUNDATION STONE
WAS LAID BY
PATIENCE & ELLA TROUT. O.B.E
DEC^R 22ND 1923
ARCHITECT
C.B. PERROTT.
BUILDERS.
BLAKE BROS.

Of the four Trout sisters, Clara was the only one to marry. Patience was the first to die, suddenly in 1949, after returning from a productive fishing trip in Start Bay. Her sisters carried on the business but Ella, too, passed away suddenly in 1952 at the age of just 54. Edith Trout, along with Gertrude, a German cook, struggled to maintain the business, which then entered a period of decline. Gertrude decided to quit in 1958, and Edith, unable to cope, closed it in 1959. For 17 years, until her death in 1975, she led the life of a recluse, living without the amenities of electricity or a piped water supply.

Following Edith's death the property was acquired by the Rose-Price family, who converted the premises into holiday flats.

These apartments continue to provide accommodation for those visiting this southern end of Start Bay. Dennis and Jill Norman took over the reins in the mid-1990s, but sadly Dennis died. Jill carried on the business and has taken a great interest in the story of Hallsands. Her folder of press cuttings and photos includes many sent to her by those who spent holidays at Hallsands many years ago.

One of the more amusing anecdotes to be recounted from those times, when the Trout girls ran the hotel, is that if the fishing nets needed to be hauled in, following a good catch, the hotel's guests were expected to leave the dining table to assist in the exercise – even if halfway through being served!

Now the building boasts a servery on its south side. In the summer season a range of refreshments are available to visitors and walkers exploring the coastline. For those heading westwards, it is the last place for refreshment for many miles.

The Hallsands Hotel was built to replace the London Inn on the rising cliff above Greenstraight. For many years it was run by Jane Knight and her close associate Edith Grellier. They had many friends in the world of show-business and signed pictures of Danny La Rue and Larry Grayson, amongst others, were displayed in the bar. They entertained many 'interesting' guests.

The hotel was bought by Carol and Dave Light, who ran it for two decades with the emphasis on diving holidays; Dave was an enthusiastic exponent of this sport. They also had their share of famous visitors, including a number of actors from *Emmerdale*. Dave died and Carol decided to sell. An auction was held in 2000 and all manner of memorabilia was sold off. At the time of writing the building stands empty awaiting demolition.

I am just about old enough to remember being taken on a tour of the ruined village of Hallsands in the 1950s. This was conducted by Miss Elizabeth Prettejohn (known as Lizzie Ann), the last resident and self-appointed guide to the original water's edge settlement. At the time, because of her wrinkled, weather-beaten face, I thought that she must have been the oldest person in the world. Although I was young, about five years old, the place also made quite a lasting impression.

Born in the Cricket Inn, at neighbouring Beesands, in 1884, Elizabeth and her family had long associations with the Start Bay shoreline. Three of her nephews had tragically drowned, two off the Start and one in the Channel. All were fishermen; none of their bodies were ever recovered.

Elizabeth kept six cats for company and also 20 fowls, which had free-range use of her home. Although one might imagine that she lived a lonely existence, this is far from the truth. Evidence that this was not the case was her annual 'haul' of Christmas cards, which came from all over the world from those she had befriended whilst touring the ruins and telling the village's story. There were also cards from those who had never visited the village, but had seen her appear on television several times and felt compelled to send their festive greetings.

She had many brothers, all buried in the parish church at Stokenham, and dedicated her life to looking after one of them, William. William Prettejohn had been obliged to leave the Merchant Navy through ill-health. He occupied himself for 44 years by making nets and sails for fishermen and Elizabeth, who never married, took care of him.

Their father was of Breton stock. He was the Philip Prettejohn mentioned earlier who bought the London Inn and, foreseeing its likely fate, wisely sold it on for £900, just in time! He then moved his wife and seven children to the house, higher than most on this rocky ledge, where Elizabeth, the youngest family member, was to spend the rest of her life. She passed away in 1964 at the age of 80.

In the late 1990s the female comedy duo French and Saunders visited Hallsands to film scenes for one of their television programmes and used the inside of Miss Prettejohn's former home.

I have been back to Hallsands many times. When I was a geography teacher in an Exeter high school, the ruins of Hallsands was a wonderful story to tell pupils – and a great excuse for a day out! We used to park the bus at Beesands and walk over Tinsey Head, continue on past the Hallsands Hotel (then on its seaward side) and at Trout's Hotel, walk down the road to visit the 'village'. How things have changed.

Cyril Courtney, who until retirement in 1995 ran the Cricket Inn with his wife Maggie, would welcome us into his pub, on our return, and regale us with first-hand accounts of these seaboard villages. On wet days he would also provide heaters so we could dry our clothes before going home. His book *Beesands and Hallsands of Yesteryear* is a must for anyone who loves this area.

The cliffs above the ruined village have continued to subside. First this resulted in the erection of this warning sign, but once the road to it became dangerous, it meant an enforced closure.

The chapel, which teeters on the edge of the cliff, now doesn't seem to have a prayer in surviving another century, though the seagulls have found it to be an extremely homely place. The once reasonable recreational space of Trout's Hotel, which ran beyond the current perimeter wall to the cliff-edge, has also disappeared.

So what of Hallsands now? One day the ruined village will disappear into oblivion, if nothing is done to resist the hand of nature. Over the years I have followed its progress with interest and I have noticed a vast reduction in the number and height of the walls of the remaining properties. The picture opposite was taken in 1976 and shows more ruins than can be seen today.

And where most of the people – bar a few who still cling to the edge of the ledge – have now long gone from the rock-ledge beneath the cliffs, very different types of person now come to hear of the village's story. One only has to look at the number of physical geography text books to see what a fine case study this is. To this end, as visitors can no longer reach the ruins, should there not be an interpretation or visitor centre of some kind to reflect this history and heritage and make their visit more fruitful? Is a viewing platform enough?

The narrow lanes leading to Hallsands ensure that it will never become another Morwellham Quay, but there is still a vast interest in the Story of Hallsands.

Fred Lynn, born in the village and related to many of those whose stories have appeared in these pages, is something of a rarity. Throughout the years he has kept newspaper cuttings and collected all sorts of memorabilia about the village. Very kindly he put this treasured material at my disposal. A man who is Hallsands through and through, it was an education to sit and listen as he reminisced about the past times of this unique village. Students by the minibus-load, even writers-a-plenty have found their way, one way or another, to his door. The only way to get the truth, as most will tell you, is from the horse's mouth!

Another fine way to appreciate the site and setting of Hallsands is to walk from Torcross, Beesands or Start Point to the village. That way the whole vista of Start Bay – the lagoons, tiny coastal villages and cliffs of various heights – will begin to convey an impression of what it must have been like to have lived here in the past.

Of course, people still do live here, but not quite as many as of yore. The days have long-since gone when school-age children went to Huckham. Today the nearest primary school is Stokenham, the parish in which both neighbouring Beesands and Hallsands lie. The closest secondary school is in Kingsbridge, not that many miles away, but a slow journey when tractors and lorries on the A379 contrive to make it seem further than it is.

When I was walking around Hallsands, during Whitsun week in 2001, I strolled past Fordworth Cottages. There were many energetic, friendly young children playing in the narrow road beneath this line of properties. They were also inquisitive about me and my two cameras. This is a picture I took, the last on the film and before some of their peers could get into view. They all looked so vibrant and so uninhibited; what an incredible place to spend a childhood!

Many of the smaller houses are now holiday homes. Who, living in any conurbation with noise and stress, wouldn't want to have a bolt-hole like this as a retreat?

This is a trend which has made humble cottages fetch a higher market price than would ordinarily be expected. Therefore it has become difficult for local young people, with low wages, to get on the housing ladder in their own patch.

On this page we have 'before and after' pictures of just one of the clifftop houses set well back from the precipice. They show what a lick of paint and a little landscaping can do to the appearance of a property. The front garden no longer resembles a school playground.

Had the dredging not taken place, would Hallsands have remained intact and survived the storms of 1951, 1979 and so on? Some of the locals with whom I talked were of the opinion that Hallsands was less exposed to the south-easterlies than the neighbouring coastal villages to the immediate north and that it might well have survived.

But what would it be like now? Would it be like Beesands, with a single pub and a significant proportion of holiday homes? We'll never know. In some ways, albeit the wrong ones, it is the destruction of its houses which has, ironically, put Hallsands on the map.